St. George

to the city that stole my heart, replaced it with
sunsets and sunrises, and made me believe in
life again, thank you.

you showed me how to love and give myself a
second chance at everything.

    to the hotel that became my home, thank you.

        -z.k.d

249

By: Zachry K. Douglas

the sky touches me and the sunsets kiss my flesh with a kind of love
never before given to a human. the roads are littered in hope and new
beginnings. there is a story it tells with every curve and straight away.
there is blood a thousand years old that cannot be washed from the
rains. humans here have a way about them as to how they walk, talk,
and move in silence. the air is sharp with renewing energy. there is a
way of life for these people and it is contagious. maybe there is hope
for all of us after all. maybe it is possible to find everything you need
only when you are lost. i feel hands carved out of the very stone out
in front of me. the most authentic soul comes from mother earth
and is granted treasures once you earn your keep, by being open
and accepting to change.

this morning woke me with the moon still beside me and the sky fresh with peace and love. the breeze opened my door, giving me the remaining portion of my dream. there is a feeling of promise and respect amongst the birds outside my window. they come from the mountains with a message of gratitude taken from the sun. where there is truth, you will find your heart beating for it. where there is love, you will feel your body aching for it.

~where there is both, you will find yourself~

the reason we exist is not to find
something, but rather to become
someone finding a home within
our broken bones.

the trickle of springs surround
me and allows me to feel the
knowledge raging below
earth's honesty.

i am not sure where this will take me, but i am made for walking and wandering this landscape as merely a visitor; nothing more.

my face no longer sags below the horizon. my eyes no longer close with fear. my hands no longer feel the need to let go. my feet press into the earth and i am no longer a human. i am a lover of the passionate and raw beauty all around me.

i am alive.

i am living.

i am happy.

i am in love.

i am present.

i am here.

i am with you.

i am finally free.

i am me.

we love like it's all we know and all we were meant for. if that is my life

and if that is the life we will keep making, please, my love, never stop

touching me. we are the ones who finally found the meaning to life.

for once you discover your hunger for something more than flesh and

words, you will never be full off of anything else as long as you're alive.

we only go as far as our aspirations. i hope you can allow the heartache

and pain to enliven you and not destroy who you want to become. life is

simple; you choose your own path or you give others the burden to show

you when you feel as if you can't do it anymore.

i've hurt more people than i have loved.

i am forever broken, but even the cracks

give way to love if it is honest.

love finds those who have been living in fragments even if you cannot piece it all together.

~love remains patient to the restless~

i fear not being able to live up to my own standards.

but then again, the pain keeps me going and gives me

strength. without it, my art would suffer.

i have ruined those who've tried to help me. i am the worst person to try and figure out. one day i am thunder, the next day i am a goddamn hurricane.

when you feel lost, open your door and look up, down, and all around.

there is always a piece that needs your soul. there is always that chance to discover what has been waiting for you today. just don't wait until it's three years later or even five. make your own fate, today.

alcohol was not only my escape, it was my reason for getting out of bed.
the first taste swallowing my soul was better than any part of my day.
i knew i was at least eight away from being someone else. that was my
life for half of my existence. that was how i functioned and saw myself.
that is how i managed my anger, depression, guilt, and shame.

back then, i was not myself until i could not control who i was.

being honest was never my thing.
i always hated hurting someone's
feelings, so i locked away how i
felt in order to keep the peace.

i would rather suffer than allow anyone to feel what i did.

i've never been good at any one thing.
i tend to fuck everything up in the end.
the difference between me and the next,
is that i am at least open about who i am
and who i am not.

i loved you so much that i forgot to save any for myself.
i forgot how to care for my wounds. i forgot how to
embrace the faceless boy i was. i forgot we all need
some type of comfort before handing it out to those
who don't know how to give you it in return.

i gave up on myself before my parents gave up on each
other. even if i tried salvaging anything that remained,
my hands had been born empty and only made to give.

you are going to feel regret sooner rather than later.
you might as well fill up your life with as many memories
as you can before all you have left to show for who you
are is just a number beside your name in the obituary.

i am looking for nothing.
i am looking for everything.
i am only confused by the
days i feel numb.

i am learning how to draw my
face and body again, so i know
where the smile goes and
where the heart should be.

maybe being content with your passion is why you are constantly running after what will kill you. you aren't afraid of being pushed past your limits, because even you do not know what they are. you are investing in an empty hole, expecting flowers to rise and kiss the moon. maybe dreamers can do that, but you have to be willing to sacrifice part of your future for anything substantial to bloom where there is nothing to begin with.

you ask for honesty and then you're upset with what i tell you. life isn't supposed to confound the one you love the most. if it's not what you want to hear, you might need to find someone who can provide you truth without being truthful.

i'd rather go broke for what i believe in than spend my money on what will never satisfy me. i've never known wealth, but i have known a few nights that never turned into day. may the money i make, no matter the amount, always bring me to places instead of purchasing things no one really needs. give me a dollar and i will show you the difference in four quarters and one hundred pennies. i don't spend money on material things that often, because in the end, nothing says more about a human than the few things in their life which they chose to keep.

i've never thought of myself to be better than anyone. i've tried to do the right thing and hope it would lead me to something greater. it didn't always go the right way, but i still learned a lesson to pass on to someone else who was struggling like i was.

even if we don't work out, i found a piece of myself
i never knew existed out here. for that, i thank you.

you brought me closer to the truth and realization
that wherever we go as individuals, our most
rewarding victories come from the tiny
battles we win between the little voice in
our heads.

the voice that screams at us, telling us we will never
make it. the voice that has kept me up past the age
of thirty trying to defeat.

                                              you silenced the noise and
                                              gave my skull a new place
                                              to plant self-love.

i feel like i am on cocaine and cannot stop typing. i was raised by lying and deceit. it was my self-defense mechanism when my reality began to shrink. i have become an expert at it and a horrible person because of it. i don't know how to stop pouring gasoline on an open flame or eating dynamite to cure my appetite for destruction. i have a wolf and lion in me, both begging to be fed. i throw them empty plates to starve each one, so my dreams can feed.

i was a terrible drunk. i always
blamed others for shit that i did
and was constantly looking for
a fight.

there was alcohol running through
my veins when i was born. all it took
was a dysfunctional household to
stir the toxicity flowing in me.

i sleep to avoid ruining the moon anymore than
i need to. she is too genuine for my rottenness.
she is too kind for my antics. she is in the sky,
and i, i am forever grounded by the hatred i
have for myself at times.

    she is where all the love comes from
    and where all seekers of light hope
    to be forgiven.

i don't know what hurts more, not seeing you

or having to leave. at this point in my trip,

both are realities i don't want to see

come true.

today is my sixth full day here. i am eternally in love with this place. it reminds me of your heart. the way everything forms into a new beginning. each turn that leads me closer to you. this is an exact replica of who you are as a woman and someone i will never stop loving.

i am not sure
where these
roads will
take us,

but i do know
now how to
get back to
you.

being on my own feels like i am still looking for my own world.

somewhere i belong.
somewhere that can
surpass my ability to
dream.

i feel like an outcast who has been sentenced to life without knowing how many doors actually open and how many visitors will come to see me. as long as there is light, my body, mind, and spirit will never die. the names etched on the walls will be a reminder to me that the only cell we keep, is the one we lock ourselves in when we feel the world around us closing in.

i am somewhat confused as to
what you want from me, from
us.

i am doing the best i can at interpreting this space i feel.

there's not a lot i have gotten right in this world. but somehow i found my way to you. every day seems like i am finally doing all the things i never could before. we go through the bullshit to grow through the realness of what life truly is. our hearts break for the sole purpose of persevering through the madness to come out beating louder for the things that truly matter.

it doesn't matter what i do,

i still cannot stop time from

taking you away from me.

eating alone in places has intrigued
me more than most of the dates i
have taken out. there is always
something new to learn about
who you are and what makes
humans, human.

even in a hotel room, i make my bed. i do anything that will set me up for success and ahead of those who take the easy approach to life.

>my intentions are to do the
>impossible before you do
>the ordinary.

even in the dark,
we find the hand
of the other
without opening
our eyes.

our connection begins as soon
as our souls face each other.

it was never about needing you more.
it was about making sure you knew i
could never give myself to anyone
else and not think about you.

i am caught between the sun
and mountains. i am afraid i
will never leave, but with my
anxiousness of potentially
going,

the possibility of seeing you
again gives my wings the
structure they need.

i don't know why it's so difficult telling people how you feel without them hating you for not saying the right thing. i guess it is easier for those who already hate themselves.

i was never one to follow rules. i hated authority. growing up without it and when it was present, it was more out of punishment than it was a teaching tool. being a middle child, i felt it was my responsibility to make sure everyone was okay before i was, or maybe, i was attempting to be both parents while they were being children about telling the truth. i was twelve going on thirty before my next birthday. i put pressure on myself that no kid needs. my burdens caught up with me and that is when my drinking became a crutch. i thought if i could escape just long enough, people would forget i was there.

i sit in this booth and look around at all the smiles and wonder why it's so goddamn hard being that happy. i think i am a good person. all i ever wanted was someone who wanted to be with me and laugh because there was no other emotion needed.

pain is being ten minutes way from someone and it feels like they are a million miles away from you. being close doesn't mean a goddamn thing if they aren't willing to meet you halfway after driving twenty one hours to see them.

we are given this life to create
a new one for the future. if you
are unable to fight for yours,
you are going to die in the past.

i am tired of ripping my
heart out for someone
who won't even show
me theirs or tell me
what they feel when
they see mine
breathing in
my hand.

i don't know what's worst:

running away from something or running to something that in the end doesn't want you. at this point in my life, both feel like my skeleton was torn out of me.

i drove around a little bit today. i saw the shadows where i once stood as a child when i was born. the sun was my father and my mother was the road. the devil stopped and asked me for directions and i told him there is nothing here for you anymore. i saw him get picked up by someone on their way to the mountains. i can't explain the aftermath. i can barely pick up my body on any given day. but driving gives me hope that my destination will have a good woman waiting to hear how my scars saved me.

i guess the next time i hear your voice, it will be to tell me if you want a life with me or thank me for visiting and go on with your own way of living. i am hoping there is not a pause. please don't let there be a fucking pause. i am too old for hesitation.

the next few days will determine
if we make it, or if we are just
another tragic tale of what
could have been.

we are trying to piece together who we are with who we want to be.

things like that only work if you are willing to forfeit part of your

heart for a chance at tomorrow.

love is only visible to those who choose to see souls instead of flesh. it teaches us how to become engaged with learning how to be vulnerable.

i came here not knowing anything about you.
i am leaving knowing less. i am leaving
knowing only why i came.

life is only fair to those who risk their hearts for the greater good of their own story. the universe shows kindness to those who kiss the stars.

you have too much love to give to allow someone the opportunity
to show none to you when you've given your best effort for them.

don't leave your hands out when their hands are already gone.

don't look at me and think you want
to be with me, when you can hardly
move your body enough to see
me.

i found what i was looking for even if it was without you.
being here has taught me to never chase those who find
it difficult to walk with you after you've ran towards
them with everything you had to be with them.

actions will always lead to the truth when you believed words
that couldn't carry anything more than an empty voice.

i left with most of my belongings. i packed all of my socks and boxers. i packed the shirts i thought i would need. i brought my typewriter and computers. my books i never opened, just nightstand worthy. i stopped six times to get fuel. i stopped six times to get snacks. i drove one thousand three hundred and ninety-three miles. i drove twenty-one hours. i got here not knowing anything about this place, but slowly morphed myself into a resident of this city. i got lost four times. i ate a different restaurant every night. i am going on three years of sobriety. four years without a cigarette. i am on my seventh day here and find myself typing until my goddamn fingers bleed, desperately looking for more words, more feelings, more adventures. looking for the perfect set and combination of words that will give me clarity as to where i go and what i will do from here. what we do with our time is nothing compared to who we give it to.

i am scared i will never be able to give you what you're looking for. i am scared i will never overcome this pain in my heart. after everything i've been through, i am thankful it still works. there are days where i wish i could place it in your body so you could feel what you mean to me and how fucking excruciating it gets on the left side of my ribs when i am scared you don't love me the same as i love you. maybe that is a sign as to what i should do, but to be honest, i don't want anyone else to have this music box except you. it has and will always play for you.

i am sure i will be back. when a place holds you like this city has and the views keep you safe, there is nothing else to do but surrender who you've been and embrace the change taking place inside.

>we travel to find pieces of ourselves. rarely do you discover a completed version of who you've wanted to be. i am scared as hell, but i believe that is what it takes if you ever want to make something of yourself. even if you go broke, fucking do it with style.

i'm going to miss this place. the weather. the people. the colors. the food. i hope to take a little piece of each thing back home to guide me in my days and months to come. i sincerely do not want to leave, but i have to figure a few things out when i make it back so i can form a better effort next time i come this way. but the good thing is, i have time to figure it out and a good woman to love. two of the greatest things one can have during a lifetime.

i walked through a graveyard today. it was humbling to see the site
where so many call home. early deaths. late in life deaths. premature
deaths. seemed like every other marker was a navy or army veteran
of wwi or wwii. i walked up and down twice and noticed most of the
graves didn't have flowers. the only people out there were the yard
crew tending to the grass and weeds. i wonder how often they get
visitors. i wonder when the last time the stone was touched by a
loved one. i walked through a graveyard to feel alive and to
understand fully just how fragile this place is. i felt the vibe
and energy from the earth and it was a sobering one to say
the least. every five or ten feet i felt something different.
i left more grounded. i don't walk through grave sites,
but this particular time it walked through me. i found
life where the dead sleep.

i wandered off by myself last night. i never left my bed, but i
was roaming the streets outside. the traffic was at a steady
pace. the lights were in sync. the homes all had their doors
closed and locked. i walked by who i was a few times to
make sure i never returned to who that man was. i awoke
still half-asleep and sweating from the sunny sky above me.

my mouth felt like i had sand between my teeth. my bones were
poking through my skin. i was transforming into something more
than human, but less of the pile of nerves i had been. i got up,
got dressed, and went about my day without the parts i needed.
the decay. the rebirth. the acknowledgement of someone i was
finally proud of.

maybe all i'll ever be is a wannabe with a curse to write until all he has left are filled journals with words no one wants to read. maybe i will be someone who has nothing left to say and alone with empty pages to burn to keep me warm. but just maybe, i can save a life before that happens by giving mine to this page.

i almost killed myself because i couldn't see a way out of the madness i had created. don't be like me. there is always a way. sometimes it takes more than a deep breath. sometimes it's riding out the storm, standing firm and tied off to your lightning rod. don't be like me. there is always a better way. there is always an out that doesn't include ending your own life. this world needs more light. not another six feet of darkness.

i have been looking for the perfect words.

                              then i waited for you to speak.

all this time being away from home has taught me that
you don't need to travel to be happy. you just need an
inner peace that can sustain you until you are ready to
go in your own direction. the current life you live is for
a reason. use it to strengthen who you are for the
moments that will defy you later in life, and then go from
there. whatever it is you are after has been looking for
you since you were born. there is a reason why we ache
for things we don't have. there was a time when they
were already within our grasp and taken away in order
for us to grow. take your time with who you are. be gentle
with your surroundings. we are all going to end up with the
same outcome. some are just better prepared and equipped
to manage what happens in-between the beginning and end.

we remember in order to feel. whatever that is, you must hold it and
nurture it to get back what you lost. and to know it's okay to hurt in
the process. nothing will ever feel as awful as the moment you realize
nothing truly has power over you. we confuse lessons with punishments.

hold anything you love close to your soul.
allow it to bloom underneath your flesh.
allow it to be raised in your lungs and
watered by the stars. the universe will
never stop growing as long as you stay
patient with the changing of seasons
taking place inside your bones.

the reason i don't ask you why, is because i'd rather not have my body crushed anymore than it needs to be. your silence gives me the answer i already know. i guess i am saving you the trouble and protecting the other parts of me that are still in shock. i have been this way since i was a kid. i never wanted to learn the truth. i'd rather die slowly than have you shoot me in the back of the head. sometimes all you can do is save yourself the pain if you just leave what they are forcing you to do. no one always gets every answer they are looking for, but it is a motherfucker when you believed the lies they tucked underneath your pillow, hoping you still believed in magic. and before i go, i just wanted to say, fuck you, and magic still exists.

i still don't know who you are, who we are. i keep hoping the next day will bring answers, but it keeps slapping me in the face with the backhand of tomorrow. to say it is frustrating would be me lying my skin off my bones. i have been shedding days off my life, worrying i have done something wrong. but in reality, it is you that hasn't done a goddamn thing since i have been here. you say you love me. you say you need me. you say and say and say until there is doubt choking who i want us to be. that's the problem. i am the only one fucking trying. i guess this is where i say goodbye and thank you for showing me why trust is one big fucking shit-show.

you got your wish wanting to date a poet. i will be sure you live a long time and feel every fucking key stroke of pain you caused me. you will feel the unbearable ache, and when i am done, you will never want to read a single line of poetry ever again. you gave me the casket. remember that.

over these mountains to the west of me is where you live, but i have yet to love you in the way i am needing. i have yet to see you in your element. i have yet to feel you in the morning. i have yet to taste you at sunset and devour you at sunrise. i guess some things will forever have boundaries no one can cross. i guess some people are just meant to be stars and some are made to be strangers in a city divided by the objects we love the most. over these mountains in front of me is where you live, and i, just a hitchhiker with his thumbs out in the wind, looking for another home to call his own.

it's funny who we are willing to love when the other person is only able to stay in their comfort zone. there is a greater pain than death. there is a greater grief than loss. some find the combination when you chase after something that loves to run away from anything remotely close to love. you can grieve the living. you can lose the alive. you can search until your body can no longer hold its bones. don't die for someone who has never held life the way you do. never let them kill you from a distance. when you get the chance, let them go and allow them to feel the fall for themselves. that's the only way they will know love as you do. after that, go on your own way. they aren't for you. you have too much soul for humans who have no heart.

it's quiet here today. most of the occupants left this morning when the rain hit. i am going to stay another week here. i need this time away and with you to figure out the next chapter of my life. hopefully the next chapter of our life. the sun broke through and it feels like i have as well. i found a place where i belong. i found a pair of arms where i belong. i found the biggest reason to be here and she is the greatest gift to ever grace the flesh of this earth. i finally found someone i don't want to run from. she is someone i want to smile with on cloudy days and get lost with under the sheets of the bed we just made. here is where i am. here is where i never saw before. here is my forever, and now.

our togetherness is what keeps the sky from falling around us.
it's what keeps the stars on our side. it's the oceans and rivers
and lakes combining all of their efforts to allow us the magic
we need to believe in a miracle never before seen by humans.
they will talk about us as lovers, and we will silently agree,
until our bodies burst with wild from the seams.

the night hits me in the heart
with such gentleness, by the
time i realize it, my eyes have
drifted behind my dreams and
i am blinded with love.

i love you for all of the ways
you tell me it's going to be
okay, and for the first time
in my life, i believe it.

we are greater than what tries to hold us back. even if it is your heart, push forward. even if it is your mind, push forward. even if it is your body, push forward, and keep your wings pointed towards the universe and go, go, go.

the only cure for loneliness is to love yourself more. love it when it cries. love it when all it wants to do is sleep. love it when you feel as if you're on empty. learn to fill your own heart, and you will out-chase every thought you have of giving up.

money only solves the problems humans don't have the heart to face.

of course it is a necessity, but don't allow it to make your soul poor

and homeless.

not everything will go as you plan. so be
prepared to change your course and
cross over the horizon when it is
necessary. do not be a creature of
habit. those things are known to kill
even the strongest of warriors.

take your sword out and carve out
the light you need. carry it with you
into the darkness and battle those
who said you'd never get to where
they are.

as long as you have some fight left in you,
you can have any fucking thing you wish.

we are the blood spilled and the teeth lost while fighting for our own life. bruises only change color once you begin to heal. take your shots and get your rest. legends never learned victory by winning every battle. they became it by outlasting those who thought they had already won.

i knew you were the one when
you gathered the heap of bones
you saw and created a human
who only needed a handful of
love.

i've never been able to provide
anyone with anything more than
words. then you came along and
heard them and made poetry
out of chaos.

the mountains speak to the soul of the earth.

how else would the sky get its color.

we talk as if the distance cannot
determine the outcome of what
we want.

the totality of what we are after,
will make the earth shift and
create space for who we will
become, together.

the moment i saw you,
every bit of life made
sense. it was as if the
scars led me to you.

now, i am healed. now, i am
well on my way to you, to us,
to the uninterrupted magic.

we haven't had that much time together, but i know forever
when i look at you and see you smile as if today was the
greatest gift to ever welcome in a love that knows
what it means to live for the other.

there is you and then there is us. nothing more will ever have my full attention like the way you have it. nothing more will ever have me as i am now, as i am yours without any reluctance or pause in my lungs. there is only you and the eyes you see me through. there is us, and the soul we share. that is how i know this to be true. you and i are moon watchers of our own sky.

when i am with you, there is no such thing as pain
growing inside my heart. you take the weeds out
of it and place your roots.

    each beat, we grow together. each beat,
    we taste the sun, each beat, we become
    one. when i am with you, there is no such
    thing as time. we bring our own sunsets.
    we make our own sunsets.

somewhere between the pages, these words got lost.

somewhere between the exits, i found rest.

somewhere between the miles underneath me,

i found you.

somewhere underneath these bones, you found my soul.

somewhere beyond this insane place we call imagination,

i dreamt in neon reds and midnight blue, until i discovered

the color in your eyes. now, today doesn't seem so far away.

she was never quiet about love. she spoke until her heart was visible. she loved until her feelings fell out of her words. she loved until her fingers were falling off from holding on for too long. she loved when love wasn't there. she loved everything and everyone with everything she stood for, and when it all came crashing down on her, she rebuilt. she constructed it again, and made her own sandcastle life out of the raindrops and dust left behind.

not everyone will get to know you like i do. i will never take you for granted. i will never leave you in bed alone. i will have my soul on you whenever yours is searching for mine. we are better for being us, when too many go without even knowing or having themselves.

her scars make her unstoppable.
her story makes her unforgettable.
her spirit makes her free and crazy.

she is the first breath of morning.
she is the most definite human i
know.

she helps me when the silence consumes.
she is love, and everything it should be.

her whispers make the the leaves move
during the autumn light, under a
purple moon. her orange colored
dreams mix with the blue under
her fingernails from attempting
to pull down the sky for the night
she so vehemently adored.
it was then her ideas grew
wings and took over the
responsibilities others in
her life had given up on.

she was at her best when everyone
else had already threw in their
heart and left without finishing
what they started. her mother
never raised her, but she is her
mother's child. she will tell you
how being welcomed in by strangers,
changed how she lived and fought
for who she is now.

you are the reason i wanted to give life another try. you begin my days and the night surrendered its darkness to embrace the light. you gave my body blood. you gave my limbs someone they can curl up next to when they are tired from the outside world. without you, there is no me to speak of.

she quiets my falling trees
and sleeps in my heart.

i never knew how to move
until she walked with me.

i never knew how to breathe
until she gave me her lungs.

i never knew a goddamn thing
until i saw her mind always
find a way to incorporate
a new approach to
something she already
knew.

i never knew me, but she adores
the questions i ask regarding
why she loves me.

you valued my silence when others left me for louder places.
not everyone will have your same comfort level for quiet
moments. not everyone will understand how it is where
one finds him or herself.

you saw me as i am and never asked
me to give you any more than i had.
you granted me love. you showed
me sins are just as valuable as the
human who has committed them
when change follows.

you are the scream that had been inside of me.

the release. the catalyst.

you are my understanding to everything which had tried to derail me. you are the sunny day i have heard about, but never felt.

i don't want to make everyone happy.

i just want happy to happen to you.

you've been sad for so long, you forgot how a smile feels. i am sorry you have been without something as pure and life-changing. but today, you will be given the moon for you to use as you please. it's the least i could do for asking her for this moment with you.

i would rather keep you safe before i ever feel relief.
i was made to be self-sacrificing. if i am not giving
more than the other, it feels as if I am living a life
full of injustice to myself and those around me.

i am burdened by the stars i have given away,
but with each new day, i am granted another
chance to give back to someone who has
never given me a fucking thing.

to me, that is something i will gladly keep doing.

there you've always been,
holding the constellations
for me to fathom how magic
does in fact live in the love
that finds you.

she has this way about her.
when you see her, you just
know you've been missing
out on the best parts of life.
you just know your life will
be changed for the better.

there is this wholeness about
her that creates room in my
heart for more than i ever
thought was possible to
hold. it is bursting with
wild.

i look at the moon every night

in hopes it will bring me closer

to you.

i hope it talks to you. i hope she

tells you how much it aches you

not being here.

we didn't always see eye to eye, but your stature put you in the stars, my love. we were meant to be here, directly in this moment of deciding our fates. i chose you with no expectations or theories behind why we are here. all i know is that if you go through life struggling more than you succeed, eventually the universe will place someone in your life you never saw coming and make them become the beautiful ending in what was a never-ending bout with loss and regret.

there seemed to be another world

existing within her. i cannot explain

her presence any more than always

having what i needed, when i did not

have the strength to ask.

she doesn't mind sharing her scars. her battles have been documented by those who have lost and no longer feel the urge to continue to push her to her threshold. there is no ceiling for this warrior. her faith remains built around the idea that everything comes from the cosmos and oceans around us. it is why she loves all seasons as much as much as the dead months in-between when love is called off due to the lack of commitment. but she is never without the love for herself. her back is marked with memories of how life used to be before becoming human, and it is what sets her apart from the crowd. she knows how much life it takes before it becomes meaningful. she knows how big the sky is and where the best viewing is for the colors she adores. she never forgot where she came from before this life. how else would she know how to fly.

i can taste you in the air around me.

women like you tend to smell of

moonlight and merlot.

just enough of both to keep the

night sober.

the desire i have for you, cannot be
tamed by simply having you near me.
i want to eat your flesh and use your
bones to pick you out of my mouth.
only your total consumption will
ease my ever-aching love for you.

love means being able to stay in bed because the reason is next to you. it means remaining faithful when bad times keep you up and won't allow you to venture into tomorrow alone without depression following you. it means having someone who not only wants to keep you safe, but knows how much you love adventure and tries to make each day that for you, without causing you stress or fear about their love for you. it means having a laugh and then discussing serious matters when it is time to, but knowing the spots on your body which provide the laughing music needed in order to remain human, when at times the world around you can drain the version they adore dearly. it is about making sure there is a balance that keeps both of you steady and never wavering on the things you want most aside from each other.

i write as if you are watching
every punch of the keys.

i want you to feel it as if i am
inscribing your soul for the
moon to read when you're
asleep.

i want you waking up, moaning
each word before i touch you.

i kiss the paper after i am done typing.
it's the only thing missing that i haven't
given you tonight. maybe one night it
will finally rest on your lips and i will
sleep under the same covers.

        maybe one day these words will make
        up the distance between our bodies.

goodnight, moon.

i hope the light cures the ache.
i hope you stay with me for as
long as you can. for even in my
dreams i can get lost.

i want to know what keeps you up. so i can be there to make sure you are at peace when i have to leave. your well being is the most important aspect of my life. some will say that is unhealthy, but it's the way it has to be if i am going to be loved by myself.

she carries flowers around with her wherever she goes. there is something about life in your hands that brings a new perspective to death and the reality of everything you touch. has the finite expiration no one will ever know, but we all understand.

she wears socks every day. not just any kind, but her happy kind. if she had it her way, she would give everyone a pair, and i believe it would not only change us, but the world. for when you love something as simple as socks, life just feels better.

when i look at you, i know why the moon
kisses you and why the sun gives you
his full attention. to be able to have
both in the same sky at once,
makes me a believer in all
things wild and unpredictable.

i could curl up next to you for the rest of my life. the thing i want most, has a name i never want to tire of saying. she gives me meaning in at times a meaningless world. she is still getting to know me, but even before we met, we shared the same heart.

you and i will make it, because you cannot go more than a lifetime without your heart outside of your chest and no one see it. but then again, all it takes is one set of eyes to ruin you for life. i will wish in the days and months to come that your touch will be the only thing that gives me life, while holding your soul to mine, so they can have the love they have been without since the stars exploded last time.

the sun hits me and i am born

again. fueling my rage for

anything resembling love.

i go in search of my lady.

you will never be without me.
a love like this has been
tested before and it
birthed the sun
and moon.

>	maybe we will have our own
>	day in the same sky.

>	maybe we have always had it.

she was like watching the sun rise during
a sunset; something never before seen.

someone unlike any magical creature you
thought you had learned about.

she was like walking on water and breathing
in a wildness unknown to this place.

she is the flower blooming in the dead of
winter.

~her bones are married to my bones~

i fell in love with an adventure which never let me go. her hair is blonde. she has a few tattoos. she runs like summer chasing fall. her daughter has magic flowing through her fingers which leads to the most awe-inspiring art you will ever see. she has two dogs who bring their own personality to each encounter with a hint of protector. she lives here. she loves here. she dreams more than she is awake. her touch is that of the top sheet of water on a clam day. she walks forward and towards her next challenge, never forgetting why she is here. her life makes me want to be a part of hers. her life is the reason the sun touches me to awake whatever parts had been sleeping. she is the open door in front of me that never closes.

tomorrow the sun will rise
and kiss the mountains and
we will be together.

that is all i know and all i
have known since your
body became my
religion.

when you awake,
allow your dreams
to hold you to the
fire and press your
soul to the stars.
until you are flat
against the truth,
you will never see
reality the way it
was meant to be
lived.

we are all worthy of a capable love.
we are destined for feelings of
something attainable to reach us
at inopportune moments to direct
our hearts to where we should be
and what inevitably matters the
most.

where we go is not a mistake. what we do when we arrive is up to us. never fault a detour for a delay in your process. it is there to give you direction, not hatred for your own life and the conflict you may find yourself in.

regardless of where you find you yourself, two breaths have been known to save a life. breathe in more than a reason to quit. breathe in more than an idea. become the breath that gives life to your lungs and fills you with the utmost respect for your journey.

there are poets,
then there are
those who just
write to feel
heard and
feel to be alive.

we are all writers.
we are all magic.
we are all more
than human if
we believe in
our powers
to heal, love,
and change.

i am sober by choice and my choices haven't always been the best to
speak of. i am a humble man and even hate speaking about it, because
i am not better than anyone else. i am no greater than you. i made a
decision that was best for me and the longevity of my own life. i was
going down a path that was clearly marked as a short lifespan.
it almost killed me once before. i speak on this subject because it is
the most important thing i can convey at this time. we don't speak
about it enough; the mental diseases. the addictions. the emotions
of it all. we wait and wait and wait until it's too late. my life was a
disease to everyone around me. i don't have a lot friends. my best
friends are no longer there for me. i have a few i can call that, but
i have separated myself from most because of my lifestyle to not
be the guy who gets wasted or needs a beer to talk about life. i am
a simple man, though some would argue i am the most complex they
have ever met, and for so long, i allowed others to rummage through
and pollute it with negativity. i never gave myself the chance to
succeed. i am now doing what i love and what keeps me going. i could
sit in this chair all day and pour my guts out to whomever is reading
this, and would feel more accomplished about that than anything i
have done in the last ten years of my life. i am myself when i am
being honest with the paper.

until we know ourselves, everyone will remain faceless. we need time to figure out who we are. for some people it takes years. for others it takes decades. do not give someone the power to tell you who you are when you have no fucking clue yourself. be dedicated in your pursuit and never accept a half-hearted effort for the things you love and take seriously. those things matter to you and they should always matter to those who care for you.

up here the sky breathes you in.
for the purest of souls can be
found howling at the top of
mountains.

they have a way of sculpting
the most broken and rebuilding
what you thought had been
torn down by someone or
people you put above your
own belief for who you are.

they cleanse you with their rigidness.

there are people
you meet and you
just know love will
bring you together
for something special.

for something you have
been without your entire
lifetime. they will make
sure they don't change a
goddamn thing about you,
but only intensify the
respect you should have
for your own life.

nothing hurts as bad as expectation versus reality.
it is one the most deadliest killers living today.
what makes it damn near impossible to stop, is
our unwillingness to accept that maybe who
we are with, is not the one we were meant
to spend forever holding.

there's more to life than the times you find yourself alone. create your own adventure.

being alone is the greatest form of love if used the right way.

being alone makes honesty the clear-cut choice in a world full of options.

the view from this vantage point, makes you see yourself as the houses, passing cars, and falling rocks. it makes you just another human who cares about his soul when others are aimlessly pretending to be full off of the bullshit they get fed on a daily basis.

the only love that exists,
is the love you carry for
the one who gives you
stars without having
to hide your light.

the way to someone's heart
is holding it with both hands
before speaking of love.

only then will it let go of the
pain and reluctance to be
open for you and able to
hear the words you have
to say.

<u>today is the perfect day to love yourself more</u>

this is what i learned from my trip and what
i thought most about while i was out there.
it provided me peace while maintaining an
adventurous approach to the life i was
looking for while being on my own.

here are to the days the sun never stops kissing the moon.
here are to the incessant days of confiding to the one you
love just how much you need them and what they mean to
you. there is never enough that can be said if who you love
is the one you want to spend eternity with, creating
and experiencing a meaningful life. here are to the days
where it won't be easy. here are to the nights where it
will feel as if living is only sought after by those who
take their skin off before laying down with only your
bones feeling the sheets. here are to eyes remaining
open that only blink to catch a breath.

at the end of the night, i look at you and know the sun will rise again.
i know my feet will dig into the earth and find strength. i know my
hands will be full of the light exploding from your fingertips.
everything has the ability to rise again, once you are being
lifted by love.

we don't understand why until we realize it was never a question to
begin with. statements made are largely engrossed with skepticism
and disbelief because of who is saying them. in most cases, after
hearing what your soul needed, you know, and long before that
you knew. we rather hide behind the false sense of security than
remove ourselves from where we know we don't belong in order
to not be alone, again.

we give the love we want,
but all too often are
forced to leave,
because they
fall grossly
short of
what we
expect.

we ache for love
because it's what
we are told about
life that saves us
from the hell we
get trapped in
when we are
afraid of giving
more than we
have.

the only life worthy of being called a life,
is that of one which gives us meaning
and purpose beyond the words we
want to hear.

the sun never sets and the moon

is never not full for those who

dream of better days.

the brave understand pain because
it is what keeps them alive. they are
not afraid of confronting it.

they welcome it and invite the magic
others swear doesn't exist from the
wound itself.

we are all chasing after our own hearts.
a testament to the will we have and a
death sentence for those who give up
long before their hearts do.

two souls destined for the other, they searched
lifetimes to find love. they searched black holes
for a chance at coming out of the other-side
with something more than finding a dead end.
until they finally found purpose for their
journey, each one continued on without giving
any thought of letting go of the flame guiding
them on their travels. before the next change
and shift of the universe, one of them was
given a star from the moon as a beacon of
promise. the moon never asked for anything
in return. she felt the urge to help after
watching their love on display and the
accumulation of rejection both had felt
over their time in space. on that night,
they both arrived together under the
same sky, and the sun welcomed in
a new found passion for his own
search of the undying adoration
between he and his lost love.

i woke up this morning thankful for being able to see another sunrise. thankful to breathe in more of this profound place of earth i am visiting. thankful for all the words i have been able to write since being here. thankful to be experiencing this life-shift i am a part of. it's a gorgeous day here. sunny, a few random clouds stopping by, with a high expected to be seventy degrees. i don't know when i am leaving. i came here not knowing anything to be honest about this trip other than trying to learn more about who i am and what my soul needs. the hotel is quiet today. three vehicles in the parking lot of my part of the hotel, including my own. i am working on two new poetry books. one of which i finished last night. it will be released as soon as i get back and get it together. i don't want to relinquish this freedom. this feeling. this magic that exists between the mountains and who i am now. i have learned more patience. i have learned to slow down more so than ever before. i am taking a full slide-show of my existence back with me whenever i feel it is time to do so. until then, this walkabout i am taking part in shall be my home for however long i feel is necessary to conclude my visit. to the places that bring out the soul in you, may you stumble upon them often.

this place has a hold on me and won't let me go. to be honest, i don't want to let go of it either. never have i been somewhere that has had so much soul and life. whether it's getting lost in thought, walking around town, looking out my door, it has me more than any place ever has. i am happy. i am at peace. i am home. i am present in everything i do. to the adventures that change your life, may you find yours embracing you each day.

until your soul tastes the wild, you will never understand the stars.
you will never understand the roads on which you travel. you will
never be settled or optimistic about anything life gives you.
you will never be open to the feeling of being alive while those
around you continually claim to know what life is about and
showing you by wasting theirs on unrealistic expectations of
never getting to where they were made for. the only limits we
have, are the ones others showcase for us on a daily basis,
which ultimately scare us off of our path.

we are the madness and the reason our hearts beg for adventure. give it what it needs. it never asks anything from you. it simply beats in hopes of you finding new ways to love and appreciate the blood giving you opportunities to live again, and again.

the world knows who has the soul
it needs to keep spinning. may you
always have the same ability.

may you never have to question
motive or reasons behind why
someone does something out
of character for you.

you will know when the soul
comes out of you in order
to be closer to their own.

it is not a death to you.
it is a reaffirmation of
what you already knew.

the ways in which we love.
show us who we are and
who they are.

never allow someone to love
you unequally and without the
fucking passion you strive for.

there are those who feel nothing
and those who feel everything.

know how to control your powers.
know how to balance your energies.
know how to maintain your existence.

not everyone feels as you do, but they
still have the ability to love you better
than those who do.

there's nothing wrong with caring for someone and showing your true colors. i'd rather display emotion and be able to keep the one i am with than pretend nothing impacts my life and only care about my own pain.

there are only a few humans
in the world with enough light
to ignite the darkness.

~you'll always be one~

we exist to help the helpless

and give hope to the hopeless.

we are all walking miracles.

we are all someone's guide

to a better life.

she opened her heart and out feel an entire galaxy.
her rawness gave her command. her pureness
gave her reason. her vulnerability gave her
purpose. her scars gave her value.

she was more then eyeliner and lipstick.
she was the face of the moon each
night someone felt alone.

we only go as far as our dreams
can take us, and then after that,
it is up to us to decide where we
go. the outcome may not be what
we had intended,

        but the revelation provides
        us new colors to add to our
        arsenal when the darkness
        tries to cover us.

love creates the strongest humans
i've ever known. only after it is
over do we realize not every
love is the same and not
every lesson was a
mistake.

the way to your heart should be paved with stars. regardless of what you have been through, if you remain hopeful, the universe will continue to give you the galaxies you feel consumed by, hoping you can make constellations from the broken pieces of its own home.

she learned the madness was always within her bones. the ache only suffocates us if we give it more meaning than it deserves. she is not only a survivor, she is the reason the blood on her knuckles gave life to her own ambitions.

no mater what they say, you still have the ability to prove them wrong. we create who we are by choosing to be different. i hope you remain that way throughout your life.

our purpose is dictated on the ability to love ourselves. beyond that, adventure takes care of the rest. wherever you go from that point, i hope you never tire from going after the things you love the most.

the universe knows how many times we have fallen, and still, it allows us to rise again. the sweet sound of chaos is my calling to love and find love in the moments there seems to be none.

long after the final breath. our music
still plays on. our voice is timeless
and the restlessness we occasionally
feel is only there to make us work
harder for what we want from a life
that has a habit of taking anything it
wants.

she grew tired of the chaos and chose to become it herself. when it comes to making decisions for the betterment of her life, she isn't the one to try and cross. if you are not being truthful with her, she will be damn sure to make an example out of you. not by physically attacking you, but by simply showing you what happens when you thought angels only came from up above. her life has been tested before. her spirit has been attacked by those who thought it was for the taking. she didn't get this far in the world by being someone who could be manipulated by your bullshit. her character has been made by the backs who have carried more than just people looking for an easy way to get through their own troubles. she is not out to get anyone. she is out to get what is rightfully hers.

the only meaning to life is the way we live it. nothing else matters when it comes down to having everything you need in order to be successful. humans are a lot of things, but not every human is able of maintaining their desire to find such meaning.

i came back to the hotel room to write down a few things,
but instead of doing that, i observed. i saw people loving
to be alive. i saw people encouraging each other to try
harder and give a better effort. i saw families enjoying
the company of their tribe. i saw the sun talk to the
earth. i saw the moon dance with the rivers. i saw
children playing on this playground here at the hotel,
which isn't built all that well, but you couldn't tell by
their laughter. i saw trucks hauling atvs. i saw cars
hauling bicycles. i saw runners on the sidewalk
stamping their footprints into a new story. i would
get up in the morning and walk those same sidewalks
and wonder what they were thinking while running
all those miles. i wondered what their motivation
was to get up that early and make an effort to be a
better overall human that day. i incorporated what
i had previously learned in my life with what i saw
while i was on my trip. they all taught me something
different, but the love you have for life in general
and for yourself is decided well before you wake up.

i forget about who i am most days. it's not on purpose, but something i need to do to feel alive. it allows me to appreciate a different perspective while focusing in on what i need to alter or change to better fit the environment i find myself in.

speak to me in stars and i will understand your soul better.
the soul knows love, because it is the purest form
walking in this crazy world.

each morning we are given a choice.
i hope today you chose your best-self.
we don't always figure life out.
sometimes, we just need to open
our hearts to accept the universe
as it is, instead of configuring
perfection when it doesn't exist.

there is a big love for you out there. someone who will always see the good in you. we forget about our own needs until it's too late and then we blame ourselves for the outcome.

        your life.
        your rules.

you decide what stays and what goes.

the reason we break is so that we
learn how to fill the holes and
cracks ourselves.

our responsibility to love who we
are is the ultimate display of
faith.

never settle for anything that isn't
up to your own giving and
understanding.

knowing what you want is not being
conceited or selfish or arrogant.

it is knowing what means the most to you
and valuing your own goddamn needs.

never forget the pain.
for it will never forget
you.

    we die for love.
    we are reborn
    through our
    promise to
    ourselves
    to try
    again.

the soul is composed of flowers,
oceans, earth, star-stuff, and a
little bit of madness.

the life set out before us craves
our best effort. only then will
our hearts be full.

life is nothing more than finding

someone you can call a friend

that loves you beyond reason

and shows you beyond measure.

we are the brave.

we are the battle

others ran from,

and continue

running from.

be able to love yourself more during the times you feel most alone. it is there you will find how to create your next breath. it is there you will fill in the gaps between your fingers with patches of dirt and galaxies.

you and i are capable of the impossible,
because the only fear we have is the
fear of not succeeding.

on the days that seem insignificant,
those are in fact the most influential
ones whispering to us.

they always show up when we need a reminder
of where we were and how far we have come.

i want you to be happy with your life and that means living for yourself when you need to. that means letting go when you need to. that means making tough choices and surrendering to the outcome. we have the capacity for greatness and you need to believe it, too.

keep going.
keep discovering.
keep reinventing.

never become a statistic of the norm.

the universe speaks to us in
all kinds of ways, but once you
hear the silence, you will know
it is your turn to lead.

the more honest we are with
who we are and those we love,
the better off we will be at
being a complete human.

we fall short of this at times,
because we think we are
meant for something that
was never ours to begin
to with.

we look out across the barren
fields and forget we are made
of the same earth and matter,
and like the things we view as
nothing, we too, turn into
absolutely nothing.

to the bridges we have burned to light
the way to our new beginning. the sun
welcomes those who have felt the
flames and pushed on.

the trail behind us is not meant to be
traveled on. it is only there to serve
as a reminder to never retrace
what broke you.

we are the animals caught in the wild of night.
our voices ricochet off the stars, giving them
a supply of life and nobility.

we are angels of the hell we escape.
we are the dogs of war. there is
no greater fight than the one we
have with ourselves.

the mountains are there for us to climb.

they only become an obstacle if we give up.

for once you do, they will grow to keep you

in, instead of them building you into who

you need to be.

eyes that are open tend to not always see everything the heart does,

it's imperative you trust it and learn to witness things through your fourth and fifth eye, and not solely rely on the ones that deceive you more times than not.

today may be your breaking point. and if you do, break for something that you will never come back from. it is only then you will learn the strength and courage it takes to be a soul living in a human body.

i am a master of nothing,

but the universe remains

a playground for those

who love to be reckless.

we are the magic makers of the cosmos.

      half-human.
      half-worldly.
      all wild.

we forget to water our own gardens and wonder why our own leaves fall from our hearts and onto the ground for others to trample over whenever they feel the need to. drown yourself. drown it as often and as much as you want to. never surrender the power and energy you possess for a dried up excuse for someone who needs what you have. you will know who they are by the amount of effort they give themselves when others around them are asking for help.

always remain faithful to yourself when the world is screaming at you, demanding you to change. there is nothing worse than watching someone you care about having to go through life ridiculed for being different than the next. for having an opinion on who they are and what they want. for speaking when the crowd is at a hush just to listen to a moron give his take about what's best for everyone.

don't be slaughtered by the very sheep others show you to be. become enriched with soul and be fucking boastful about the identity given to you that you have fought to maintain. don't go gently. don't go quietly. don't go at all. remain in the strange and keep being someone others are unnerved by.

~nothing looks better than wearing sincerity on your heart~

be responsible with your love.

we are the single most important aspect to our life. we deserve the best and biggest love out there. it isn't to be taken lightly. it is the one thing that will wait for you, but it leaves as quickly as you found it if your intentions are to abuse it.

we suffer simply based out of fear for losing something and thinking we will never have it again. we dig our own graves long before we give ourselves a chance at survival.

i love weird things more than the normalcy
others embrace. there is something innocent
and genuine about it. there is a calm that folds
down over you and gives you satisfaction and
a new desire to find more of it.

~weird is my voice of reason~

the pain teaches us how to love ourselves
again. it teaches us as long as we feel, it
matters.

      as long as it is there, it's reminding us
      regardless of how much it hurts,
      we are alive and will be healed
      again to get back on the
      chase.

spend time doing what you love and never second guess what you need to do. what other people think will never matter to a dedicated heart.

it is there you will listen to a changed mind, but never one that is lying about the truth you are after or the life you want.

i hope you find someone who is willing to bring out the best of you, for you, with intentions as soft and delicate as the morning moon holding it all together.

you don't need anyone's permission to be who you want. your life depends on your own aspirations. start there and move forward.

begin where you have felt the most pain.

begin where it hurts to touch.

begin where you are needed and loved.

begin for who you are ready to be.

you are not imaginary. stop allowing people to make you feel that you are. the face you have was carved out of magic. the skin you wear was set upon you by the angels. there are gods living inside of you. there is immortality scorched on your fingertips. you are not a false sense of reality. you are the goddamn meaning to someone's life who cannot make out what they are supposed to be doing.

people watching is something i have always done. i look at this group
and hope i still have friends at that age. i hope they are on a road trip
as well and getting the full extent of life. maybe it's a couple's retreat.
maybe it's a birthday. maybe it's something they do every day.
whatever it is, i hope they enjoy themselves. it is a little crowded in
here, but nothing too bad. they are at the center of the room and i find
myself observing them with great joy, as they laugh and smile and drink
their coffee. ages ranging from sixties to eighties i would imagine with
maybe one or two ninety year olds mixed in. my eating schedule is that
of an old man. i have cereal, coffee, juice, and eggs most of the time
when i am on a trip. coffee always tastes better when you're traveling.
after that, i eat a small lunch or snack, and then by five o'clock i am
starving. living with my dad, i have picked up some older habits, but i
don't mind it, because i get to see life in front of me when it is time to
eat out on the road. there are a few people eating alone, including me.
i wonder why they are eating alone. i wonder where they are going.
the eight elderly eating in front of me, give me hope that age is only
a limit others put on us.

walking around this town you never know what you're going
to see the second or third time around. i saw this little guy,
a structure made from rusted and recycled iron and metal.
i thought how astounding it is to see random art all over
your town. it is everywhere out here. from constructed
mailboxes, customized vehicles, to people in general.
some new. some old. some just in the beginning stages
of becoming specialized in whatever way it needs to be.
it is seventy-three and sunny now. i am in paradise. it's
funny that i used to think the beach was the definition for
such a word. i have always been in love with nature and
being outdoors, so when you open your door or throw
open the shades and see mountains, insane sunrises
and sunsets, and vibrant everything, you get to
experience life on a deeper level. i am lucky to be
here in this moment. i am a nomad, who is half-beach
bum, but entirely secure in his own life.

today i am going to take more time to explore. i pretty much took yesterday off. i was maxed out. i have been on the go since the first of this month. it felt good to relax and have some quality time to myself. i am learning how to be selfish with my time and give more of it to my life and who i need to be. i have been giving everyone else more love and affection than i have shown myself for the better part of my life. being an empath, i am still learning how to access parts of who i am and being able to condense all of what i feel. in my twenties, i drank to keep things at bay, along with other random and formidable reasons. i was a sad excuse for a man back then. i neglected those who loved me. i shunned anyone away who tried to help. i was comfortable in my self-destruction. being out here has taught me an incredible amount of lessons and perseverance. it has taught me more patience. it's insane how quickly time passes us in the now. especially looking back at the trip in its entirety. time is only here for as long as we give it meaning. i am still learning the ins and outs of myself. i am still leaning how to breathe instead of holding it in when i am scared or uneasy. the main thing i have learned is that a fierce love for yourself will take you beyond the anxiety you feel when you're up against the unknown. today i welcome in more of it and i will keep making art the way i see, breathe, and feel it.

i've been living afraid and with uncertainty. i was raised to always believe in myself no matter the situation facing me. at times it is hard to live up to that standard. at times it is easier doing the least amount that is asked of you. playing it safe and not exploring. waiting for something to happen instead of making shit happen for yourself. i took this road trip with a few things in mind and so far i have overcome a lot of my self-doubt and anxiety about being on my own. i am human, and most of what is going on in my head is self-induced. i am relearning who i am. i am relearning what i want. i am balancing life, work, and priorities now. it feels good being on top of your mountain after settling for trails that kept you safe. explore. reach new goals. failing is only possible if you're trying. success comes shortly after. looking forward to seeing what the rest of the trip has in store for me.

this last page is dedicated to you, my love.
without you, i never would have found myself.
i would still be wandering off into some oblivion
that looked like home. now, here you are, giving
me a soul for a roof and a heart for a bed.

easy living and wild love keeps me free.

www.ingramcontent.com/pod-product-compliance
Lightning Source LLC
Chambersburg PA
CBHW032035290426
44110CB00012B/818